Split Ends and Caramel Frappuccinos
By: Ashleigh Lauryn Young

Publisher: lulu.com
Morrisville, NC

ISBN: 978-0-6151-7064-0

Introduction and note from the author:

Split Ends and Caramel Frappuccinos is a collection of every single poem that I have written in the past eight years. This book is so precious to me, because it contains all the emotions and feelings that I have dealt with all throughout my teen years. The poems include lessons in love, heartache, pain, depression, confusion, friendship, and life; everything that you learn while growing up. Some of these poems, I have written and dedicated to my close friends, because they have dealt with some of the same things. I hope you enjoy reading my poetry as much as I enjoyed writing them!

-Ashleigh Young

Split Ends
and
Caramel Frappuccinos
By: Ashleigh Lauryn Young

This book is for all the people who have inspired me to write these poems, for my wonderful fiancé Ian, and for the Lord who gave me this talent.

"You were the model of perfection; full of wisdom and perfect in beauty."
—Ezekiel 28:12

"Strength To Endure"

Strength To Endure

I've stumbled like many,
I've fallen down hard;
Faced trouble and heartache,
And let down my guard.

I've trusted to carelessly,
I've had my share of tears;
I've learned that people change,
In only a few short years.

I've learned who my friends are,
And which ones to let go;
I've learned who I trust,
And those I don't.

I've had my problems,
And I've had my doubts;
This life's thrown some curves,
But that's what it's about.

However, one things for certain,
I know this for sure;
I have what it takes,
The strength to endure.

A Cowgirl's Duty

A cowgirl has a duty,
To all her friends and family;
To treat them good and with respect,
To put them first
Then herself next.

A cowgirl has a duty
To her loyal steed;
To be patient and to be gentle,
And care for all his needs.

A cowgirl has a duty,
To the way she makes her living;
To work real hard and do her best,
For her all she must be giving.

A cowgirl has a duty,
To uphold her cowgirl name;
She must wear her hat and wear her boots,
So it won't be put to shame.

A cowgirl has a duty
To her sleeping hound
To not command him anything,
For he has short legs, and weighs fifty pounds!

If a cowgirl does her duty,
And does her duties well;
You know that she's a keeper,
By her actions you can tell.

A Knight's Death

All else faded as my vision clouded to a blurry blue.
The sword I carried grew heavier in my calloused hand, with every breath that I fought for.
The last thing I saw were thousands of men running at each other. Anger coursing through their veins.
The crimson red blood of another man stains and claims my blade and my armor.
The stench of death now hit me like never before. I fall to my knees. Shrieks of wounded horses and cries from pierced men are now a distant hum.
Everything around me slows, as if my whole life was caught up in this one moment, and I fall further to the dust from which I came.
I feel my pain, I see my death, and I die in my honor.

A Lost Sinner's Question

Jesus, Jesus, a name I often hear, and His name keeps ringing in my ear. I hear some say He's the Son of God; in church some say "Amen," and nod. So who is this Jesus they call a Savior? With all of His miracle behavior? I thought He might be just a man, but saving lost souls? Maybe He can?
I go to church every Sunday, just as I should. I did good deeds…all that I could. Maybe just maybe I'm going to Hell, but how do they know that this Jesus is real? Truly, how can they tell? But now I know why they believe in this Lord, and now I know why the Bible is called a sword. They read it and have faith in Him; they know that He'll come back again. To take up those who have been saved, and to put those down who have pushed Him away. Now it's all come clear to me, now I plainly see…that I am lost so helplessly. So Jesus, Jesus, save my soul, and keep me from falling to that dark fiery hole. Come into my heart and set me free, so that I can be a witness for Thee. Amen.

A Secret Untold

Among the statue of which she prays
In a sleeping spell she lays
Where truth goes untold
And fantasy lives
A darkest of secrets is about to give in.
Through unwanted hardship
And unwanted pain
It was a great loss
But also a gain.
And to another the sin approached
Another gain and so she wept,
A sacred secret now demands to be kept
Out of her spell, the truth is now told
All sorrow is lot
And virtue is gold.

A Sleepless World

In a world that does not sleep
Even after sleep has come;
Visions and stories unfold to some.
Sightings of the future
And happenings that are wished to occur;
Things that overwhelm us
And frighten us to be sure
Anything can happen
As it most always does.
Some visions unfold peace
And assurance for the weary
Some sightings unfold wishes
And some are very dreary.
But in a world that does not sleep
It still must come to a close
And until the day it comes to life,
New dreams remain untold.

All is Lost

All is lost,
As the red flower fades;
All is lost
As the warm heart grows cold;
All is lost
As the seasons change.
All is gone
As the sun turns to moon
All is gone
As the morning goes noon
All is gone as the dry dust settles
And the last leaf falls.
All is taken
As the sparrow breathes his last
All is taken
As the old man closes his eyes
And all is lost
As she starts to cry.

All Our Firsts

Verse 1:

I saw you walkin' on the streets today
And our past came rushin' back to me
Just as quickly as it had escaped.

And I tried to forget once again,
The warmth in your touch
And the linger in your gaze;
You lips against mine,
And how we spent all our days.

And I just couldn't forget
All our firsts in the beginning
And all our lasts in the end.

Chorus:

Like the first time we cried
The first time we danced,
The way you looked when I took your hand;
The first time we kissed,
And when I held you close,
The first time we whispered when we spoke;
The first time we laughed
And ran my fingers through your hair,
And when we fell asleep in your lazy chair.

Verse 2:

It brings tears to my eyes
To remember those times,
But it's times like these
That makes love worthwhile.

Now I'm walkin' alone on these streets
Waiting for my life to begin.
But I just can't forget
All our firsts in the beginning
And all our lasts in the end.

Chorus 2:

Like the last time we cried,
The last time we danced,
The way you looked when I released your hand.
The last time we kissed,
And I let you go,
And I tried not to let my wet eyes show.
The last time we laughed,
And ran my fingers through your hair,
The last time we fell asleep in your lazy chair.
The last time we spoke,
And I said goodbye;
And the first time I looked up and saw pain in your eyes…

Another Of Life's Chapters

I've hit that mile marker
The one where you can't turn back
And I haven't really come to terms
With how I'm supposed to feel or act

Something that I held so dear
For all these many years
Vanished in a second
And now replaced with guilt and fear

I still can't quite believe it
Even though I've gone that far
I just don't want to face it
I'm afraid I've left a scar

Since I can't go back to yesterday
I'll have to face all these tomorrows
Find pride in something else
And quit dwelling on the sorrow

Apology
(For her)

It's been four long months since I've held you
Then he came along and I fell through.
I got carried away when he called me baby,
I got too involved and no one could save me.

But I see now what I didn't see then,
That he can't make me smile like you do,
Instead he made me sin.

I'm so sorry babe, for the pain that I've caused;
I'll burn these old bridges,
And take our love off of pause.

Back at the Shores

Among the crowds,
One is full of hate,
Anger overwhelms her,
For the hurt is just too great.
Sometimes it's too hard to handle
For others have made her love a scandal.
So with a need to get away,
She closes her eyes,
All her troubles are over
And she's under clear blue skies.
Her mind wanders on
And she's sitting in the sand,
The waters rushing up
And it's touching her hands.
For now the pain is gone,
Until her vision opens,
Her sorrow come once more
Until again she's at the shore.

Back Where I Belong

Verse 1:

It's been a month and a half,
Since we've gone separate ways;
Now working all week long
Is how we spend all our days.

I used to be so strong,
Having you to lean on;
And your confidence was so much
And I have none, since your gone.

Chorus:

Yeah, I've sunk back to my level of reality,
My seventeen-year-old sanity;
I was so much more with you by my side,
I looked up to you,
And in you I confided.
Now I'm back where I started,
Lonely and confused,
I now know my place
And I wish it was back with you.

Verse 2:

Our love was so beautiful
And you were so ready,
To get out of town
And fly away with me.

But something changed
And I was searching for more;
Now I know I was foolish,
Breaking loose
And not knowing what to look for.

Chorus:

Yeah, I've sunk back to my level of reality,
My seventeen-year-old sanity;
I was so much more with you by my side,
I looked up to you,
And in you I confided.
Now I'm back where I started,
Lonely and confused,
I now know my place
And I wish it was back with you.

Burning Love

What joy is found
When love enflames you
Burning deep inside your soul.
The flicker of flames reaching up
And warming your heart grown cold.
What pleasure is found in a simple touch
And courses through your veins
The kiss that leaves you breathless
And steals your heart away.

Come Back to Me Once More
(Poem from a man to his love)

Oh my fair lady
For two fortnights have I wooed you!
Hath your heart no room for my searching soul?
I beg you let me in
And let me woo you again!
Perhaps you'll bend to my gentle ways
I've loved no other worth loving.
My fair lady
Let me once again kiss your soft sweet lips
And have pleasure if only once more,
Just to pretend that you love me.

Dancing That Night

All I can see
Is the sparkle in your eyes
As you held me close
And we danced
To a country lullaby

The taste of your lips
Your hands on my waist
We moved to the beat
A slow sexy pace

I can feel the heat
In our lustful round
My body against yours
As I move down the ground

The heavy breathing
Lingers in every sigh
The desires in your heart
Are shown here tonight

I close my eyes
As I dance to the rhythm
The tingle in his touch
And my contentment with him

The soft silky feel
The satin of my dress
You run your hands over it
In an "I want you" caress…

Distracted Distress

My pencil falls limp in my hand as I sit and stare at a page in my book. My gaze becomes unfocused and the words turn blurry as a mixture of emotions flows through my body. A chill runs down my back at my sorrowful memories. Often throughout the day, my heart brings me back to the pain. My pencil wanders off from writing equations and instead chooses to write sad poems in the margins of my page. Will my sorrow ever end? No one sees me in my anguish. I hide it behind a smile that is only meant to spare my emotions.

Don't Cry Over Me

I can't keep the rain from falling
I can't keep the sun away
I can't keep your heart from breakin'
And you couldn't make me stay.

Don't be upset
You'll see better days
You'll find someone else
Who has all the right things to say.

Just because I'm opinionated
Don't be afraid
There are other people out there
Who will bend to your ways.

Baby I'm a flower that's bloomin'
And there's nothing you can do
Can't keep a bud closed forever
Unless you break it in two.

Your gonna be just fine
So don't cry over me
There's even someone out there for you
Trust me, you'll see.

Dying Love

The flame is burning out,
The fires turned to ash;
The love is true
But I start to doubt.
His kiss is too familiar,
His touch no longer warms me,
I love him still
But how long will that be?

Everything
(For Molly)

Verse 1:

Look at that beautiful life
Trying so hard to move on
How much does it take
It just seems so wrong

She's done nothing but give
And they take it all
They break her heart
And watch her fall

Yet she still smiles
Despite all her pain
It's amazing to me
She's got so much to gain

Chorus:

She's hiding the pieces
To her broken soul
Nobody sees
Nobody knows

The day is so promising
The nights are so long
Laying alone
In those silent tear songs

I don't understand
Why's it have to be her?
She deserves everything
Everything that they were

Verse 2:

If you look in her eyes
You can see that she's crying
Her heart breaks mercilessly
Behind the smile she's smiling

She's been loved
And she's been left
She's been the victim
Of love's grand theft

I just don't see
How they can stand to leave
Her perfect love
And all they could be

Chorus:

She's hiding the pieces
To her broken soul
Nobody sees
Nobody knows

The day is so promising
The nights are so long
Laying alone
In those silent tear songs

I don't understand
Why's it have to be her?
She deserves everything
Everything that they were

Exposed

Her thoughts are so heavy today
And what she had done
Only few can say

They had each other and the night
At the tips of their fingers
The smiles the laughter
Started to linger

Her heart turns to guilt
Her mind turns to anger
Why can't they see?
There wasn't any danger

One small mistake
Brought on a war
She did nothing wrong
But they don't trust her anymore

Why won't they listen?
They don't understand
Their standards are too high
They're too much to demand

She's hurt and she's broken
Confused and exposed
They have no more mercy
No forgiveness to show

Feelings Untold

The dark time of the day
And the two are out of sight
The sun is gone
The day is done
And there's nothing left to say.
So many feelings
And so many emotions
What's done is done
And hearts are reeling.
Whispers are felt
Their containing love's thoughts
Not everyone knows
That a future's been dealt.

Fighting For Heart

This emotion I cannot hide,
The feelings run to deep;
There are problems at the present,
And it's hard for me to sleep.
Anger and pride has found their way in,
But it's not coming from me,
For he's done no sin.
Throughout the day,
My thoughts drift away;
Stress and depression,
My soul cannot say.
By today's evening hour,
My future will be shown;
I'll fight for my feelings,
Because my heart's not my own.

Finish What You Started

You can't take back
Some things that we've done
But don't try to back me out
Once you've begun

Can't you see
The confusion you've caused
We've been there before
And didn't break any laws

If your not gonna finish
All that you started
Then baby don't bother
You can't do it half hearted

If your not givin it all
Then don't waste your time
This hurt and humility
Is not worth a dime

You can't expect me to stop
Once you get me going
Your sending wrong signals
Without me even knowing

So I have to ask why
It always comes to this
And I'm always uncertain
Every time we kiss

He Can't See
(For her)

Tears are calling
Emotions are tight
She's hiding her smile
From him tonight

He created a battle
Full of lust and desire
Then left it alone
After starting the fire

The tenderness of his touch
The blue of his eyes
God, he's so beautiful
So why does she cry?

She holds him so close
So he can't get away
She fears she might lose him
If she can't make him stay

She wants to tell him
Those three simple words
But he never believes her
It's what she deserves

The softest kiss
He touches her lips
He leaves a trail
The warmth of his fingertips

The phrase is so tempting
It's stuck on her tongue
She wants him to finish
What he's begun

Her watered eyes
Hold back her pain
He caresses her cheek
As she tries to stay sane.

Hear the Earth Breathe

Walking down the narrow path, shuffling my feet in the autumn leaves, I can feel the spirits of the animals all around me. They are walking along with me in their own way, giving me comfort. Speaking to my heart. My people believe that each animal has a lesson that they can teach us. A story about their lives. The soft shyness of the deer. The bravery and solitude of the wolf, and the quiet beauty of the horse. The courage and strength of the bear. Listen closely and open your mind. You can hear the earth breathe.

Heartache it Breaks

What actions were done?
What words were said?
I don't understand,
Why did you run?
All of your dreams,
Believing them too;
Hope is all lost
And now we are through.
The illusions,
The lies,
I can't comprehend;
In darkness,
In shadows,
"I'm shattered" my heart cries.
But I'm still here,
And you still fled;
You should've save me the heartache,
You replaced it with fear.
Sensitive is it's beat,
Yet you brought it down hard;
Torn into pieces,
And thrown at my feet.
So pick it back up,
Then leave it alone;
I'll restore is all back,
And all on my own.

He's My Everything

Verse 1:

I traced his lips with my fingertips
As he peacefully slept
I lay by his side
So quiet and content

I can't begin to tell you
How I ever came this far
To deserve a love like this
That would heal all my past scars

I can see my future
Every time he takes my hand
And maybe one day
I'll wear his wedding band

Chorus:

He's the face that I wake up to
And the one when I fall asleep
He holds me to show he needs me
And holds me when I weep

I feel so safe
In his comforting arms
Nothing can reach me
And I'm free from harm

His love couldn't shine any brighter
When you looked into his eyes
He loves me like there's no tomorrow
And I really don't know why

He's my childhood fairytale wish
And all my dreams come true
He's everything I ever wanted
And everything I never knew

Verse 2:

I kiss his sleepy eyes
As I still watch him sleep
I'm still in awe
How I fell so deep

This love that I found
Still amazes me
It's so hard to believe
I mean, it's just so crazy
How:

Chorus:

He's the face that I wake up to
And the one when I fall asleep
He holds me to show he needs me
And holds me when I weep

I feel so safe
In his comforting arms
Nothing can reach me
And I'm free from harm

His love couldn't shine any brighter
When you looked into his eyes
He loves me like there's no tomorrow
And he knows he can't deny

He's my childhood fairytale wish
And all my dreams come true
He's everything I ever wanted
And everything I never knew

He's the face that I wake up to
And all my dreams come true

Hidden Behind the Mask

Day by day,
This life travels on
Once which was happy
Weeps for that which is gone.
Hour by hour
The smile's not real
But it's forced there by sorrow
Just how does it feel?
Minute by minute
This heart's still in pain
The hurt is so great
The tears leave a stain.
This broken being
Where it might be
Dying in this law
Until love is set free.

How I Want It

I wanna see the southern stars
When you look into my eyes,
They'll tell me all your secrets,
Your truths and your lies.

I wanna feel like I can fly
When you lift me up to hold me,
To taste the warmth of summer,
In a kiss as sweet as honey.

Can you help me hear the ocean?
When you whisper in my ear,
When you tell me that you love me
With no regrets or fears.

I want the thunder to roll
When you make it clear you want me,
Leaving me breathless
And I'm all that you see.

I want to feel the rush of the wind
When you reach out and touch me
It might be asking too much
But that's how I want our love to be.

How Strange is the Heart

How strange is the heart!
Today full of joy,
Tomorrow empty and sad.

How strange is the heart!
We give ours away,
And then take it back.

It's full of happiness
And full of love
Overflowing from the top
And then it's broken
And the pain won't stop.

I Ain't Making Up Tonight

Verse I:

Look at us standin' here
With anger in our eyes;
I'm mad at you for cheatin'
Your mad cause I finally caught on to your lies.

Go on
Give me your pitiful excuse;
It don't matter anyway
Cause we always play this game
And baby your gonna lose.

Chorus:

Well ya know what,
Just forget it,
Your on your own;
If your gonna act this way,
I'm probably better off alone.

You ran out of second chances
After your first chance;
So I'm walkin out that door,
I'm tired of our broken romance.

And this time I ain't cryin'
Cause it's you who's screwin' up;
Go tell someone else your sob story
Cause I'm givin' up.

Save your words for someone else's fight
Cause I ain't kissin' and makin' up tonight.

Verse II:

You say it didn't matter
You drank a little to much;
If she's not the one you love,
Then why'd you surrender to her touch?

Baby I ain't got no mercy
For the way you've treated me,
Don't bother packin' your bags
Cause I'll be more than happy to leave.

Chorus:

Well ya know what,
Just forget it,
Your on your own;
If your gonna act this way,
I'm probably better off alone.

You ran out of second chances
After your first chance;
So I'm walkin out that door,
I'm tired of our broken romance.

And this time I ain't cryin'
Cause it's you who's screwin' up;
Go tell someone else your sob story
Cause I'm givin' up.

Save your words for someone else's fight
Cause I ain't kissin' and makin' up tonight.

No I ain't kissin' you tonight
I won't be makin' up tonight

I Am Yours

Love me softly
Kiss me tender
Catch me gently
As my heart surrenders.

See me fully
Speak so strong
Whisper calmly
For you, will I long.

I can't do this anymore

Baby I'm hanging by a thread
And it's not enough to keep me
I know you've gotta see it
Don't pretend that you're not guilty

You can't expect me to hold on
To what's never comin' my way
You can't expect me to forget
All the things you never say

Your always good at playing games
And telling me I'm priceless
But honey if that were true
I'd be above all your successes

If you can't give me what I need
Then why am I still here?
I don't have to put up with this
Lord it's been a long year

Baby it's not my fault
That you have your priority's wrong
I've been set aside to often
And pushed away too long

I Don't Understand

I can't seem to grasp this
But I'm trying so hard,
I'm not used to this way,
And it's you that I miss.
Seeing you daily,
Hurts even more;
But I want you to know
You're worth waiting for.
I see you the same,
And I can't come to terms
That I can't touch your face,
And "image" is to blame.
I can't see why,
Cause your still mine,
They can keep us away,
But it won't change my mind.
So I'll keep on trying,
And we'll live this on through
It may take awhile,
But I will be with you.

I Drink to my Death

I drink to my friends,
My family and foes;
I drink to my heartache,
My pain and my woes.
At the end of the bottle
My troubles are past,
And off to the side,
My sorrow is cast.
I drink to forget,
All things worth forgetting;
I drink to my health,
My happiness and wealth.
At the end of the bottle,
Whiskey is on my breath,
And at the end of the bottle,
I drink to my death.

I Love You This Much
(Ashleigh's first love poem)

My head's above the clouds,
My heart's no longer mine;
My attention span gets lost,
Yet I think it's all just fine.
You're driving me insane,
And I don't know what to do;
I'm afraid I've lost my mind,
And it's all from loving you.
The first time I heard you cry,
My heart began to break,
And when you said you loved me,
My heart was yours to take.
So every time you hold me
And with every little touch,
I really can't explain it,
But I love you this much.

I Want to Love You

Verse 1:

Some live a lifetime and never see
The love and the passion I see in your eyes.
Your heart is true, your intensions pure;
Your love has mended all those lies.

Chorus:

I wanna give you a chance,
I wanna take a risk,
I wanna show you my heart
And I wanna be kissed.
I've been hurt before
But it won't keep me away,
So show me your love
Cause I want you to stay.

Verse 2:

The more you're around
I feel excited and free,
And my heart skips a beat
Every time you look at me.

I don't know how you do it,
But you do it just the same,
I'm drawn to you like a magnet,
And I love to say your name.

Chorus:

So, I wanna give you a chance,
I wanna take a risk,
I wanna show you my heart
And I wanna be kissed.
I've been hurt before
But it won't keep me away,
So show me your love
Cause I want you to stay.

I Want You to Know my Name

Verse I:

I open my mouth to speak
Yet nobody hears me again
My words sound like
They never leave my lips
One muted opinion
Among so many men

I write down my thoughts
And hide them away
Nobody's listened
By the end of the day

Chorus:

How can I tell them
How will they know
I have but one voice
A voice of my own
I want to be heard
To rise up and speak
Thoughts of my own
That are very unique
I don't want all the critics
Or all of the fame
I just want them to know my name

Verse II:

I'm hidden away
I'm off to the side
A small little voice
I'm denied it cried

Let me tell you my story
Of nobody worth while
Just one of many
With a beautiful smile

Chorus:

How can I tell you
How will you know

I have but one voice
A voice of my own
I want to be heard
To rise up and speak
Thoughts of my own
That are very unique
I don't want all the critics
Or all of the fame;
I just want them to know my name

I Won't Forget

Growin' up in a small town,
Makin' friends and getting down
On the weekends.

Me and you hangin' out
Talkin' trash and gettin' loud
Yeah we've had fun for four long years,
You make me whole and together we have no fears.

But now it's time for me to go
The last hour's passing
And I hope it goes by slow.
Growin' up is hard and I sure hope I'm ready,
But I'll never forget you as my life starts gettin' steady.

And I'll never forget Mexico, or the beaches down in Destin,
The boat ride in Aruba,
Lying in the sand resting.

Think of me often
As I will of you,
I know you will miss me,
Cause I'll miss you too!

If It's Not Me

Verse 1:

Today's a new day
Full of hope for this broken heart
Even in pain,
A little light is a fresh start.

Sometimes I can't help but wander,
As we live our lives through
If you've found someone else
Someone else new.

Chorus:

If it's not me,
Then who will you hold?
All your life's heartaches,
It was me that you told.

If it's not me,
Then whose arms will embrace you?
If you're not in my life
What life will you pursue?

If not me,
Then who will you love?
Will someone else's heart be enough?
I guess I'll move on
And you will too
But if it's not me,
Then who?

Verse 2:

Well I'm doin' all right
Through this heart filled fight,
But sometimes I lie awake
And think about us at night.

I'm not askin' for you back
So cut me some slack
When I ask:

Chorus:

If it's not me,
Then who will you hold?
All your life's heartaches,
It was me that you told.

If it's not me,
Then whose arms will embrace you?
If you're not in my life
What life will you pursue?

If not me,
Then who will you love?
Will someone else's heart be enough?
I guess I'll move on
And you will too
But if it's not me,
Then who?

I'll Bow Out Now

Verse 1:

I can't believe our perfect love
Slipped right through my fingers
And since we don't talk about it
The silence of it lingers.

Well I've tried to stay away
From you and your heart,
And since you act like I bother you,
I guess I'll start;
To bow out of your life
And out of your reach,
And when you start to miss me,
Remember your "moving on" speech
You gave to me.

Chorus:

Well, since you don't care
I'll bow out now,
I'll let you find love again,
Even if I don't know how.
I'll suffer to myself
In a corner in my heart
I'll bow out now.

Verse 2:

It's no use
Tryin' to show you my pain;
You ignore it anyway,
And it drives me insane.
You see right past it,
And let me die inside;
Even as I stand in this crowd,
I'm alone and I cry.

Chorus:

Well, since you don't care
I'll bow out now,
I'll let you find love again,
Even if I don't know how.
I'll suffer to myself
In a corner in my heart
I'll bow out now.

Verse 3:

I can only hope
One day to find
A love as true
As was yours and mine

I hope to be happy
As you seem to be today;
It'll take awhile,
But I'll be ok.

Chorus:

Well, since you don't care
I'll bow out now,
I'll let you find love again,
Even if I don't know how.
I'll suffer to myself
In a corner in my heart
I'll bow out now.

I'll Leave Summer Behind

Verse 1:

Well summer's almost over,
And then I'll be on my way;
Maybe things would be different
If you had chose to stay.

But I've already cried
And I've already prayed,
And I can't take back
All the tears that I've made.

Chorus:

So I'll take what's left of summer
And I'll face it with a smile;
Before I move on with the rest of my life
And walkin' all these lonely miles.
I'll think of you from time to time
And then I'll leave summer behind.

Verse 2:

I have too much to live for
And too much to work for,
To mess myself up over you;
So I'll pick myself up
And get off my knees, now that we're through.

Chorus:

So I'll take what's left of summer
And I'll face it with a smile;
Before I move on with the rest of my life
And walkin' all these lonely miles.
I'll think of you from time to time
And then I'll leave summer behind.

I'm a Fool

Verse 1:

Sitting here alone,
Thinking about you,
A tear rolls down my cheek
At the thought of us being through.

As I'm sitting here remembering
How happy we used to be,
I think about what happened that night,
And all the love we chose not to see.

Chorus:

And I'm a fool for not believing in love,
And believing I could live without it.
For thinking I could go everyday,
Without your smile,
And seeing your face.
Oh and I'm a fool for leaving you behind,
Convinced you'd be gone in the back of my mind.

Verse 2:

Hearin' your voice tonight on the phone
Brought joy to my heart
But added to the pain.
When you said goodbye with no "I love you"
I thought I'd go insane.
I don't want nobody else,
So give us one more chance;
Let's try again with our broken romance.

Chorus:

And I'm a fool for not believing in love,
And believing I could live without it.
For thinking I could go everyday,
Without your smile,
And seeing your face.
Oh and I'm a fool for leaving you behind,
Convinced you'd be gone in the back of my mind.

It's Still Pain

I'm bleeding
But no one sees,
I'm crying
But no one hears.
My eyes are full of tears,
They beg to be let go
And to fall down the cheeks of yet another victim.
My heart has ripped apart
At the sound of their tempting whispers,
As though a blade has pierced right through my soul.
My mind is swirling,
As the rest of the world flies by without ever looking back
To see who it has hurt.
Everything is happening to fast,
And I can't keep up.
It's driving me insane.
My pain won't fade
As they say it will,
My pride won't fall
As they hope it does,
My love won't fail,
As they beg it to do,
Don't play with other's hearts.

I've Been Dreaming Again

My dreams have been shattered,
They've been trampled and stepped on,
Like nothing else mattered.
I've gotten my hopes up,
Easily broken like ice;
It was too good to be true,
Happiness has a price.
We had it all planned,
Our future was made;
His thoughts are now different,
It wasn't a fair trade.
The tears came so fast,
Because it wasn't expected;
You were positive and sure
Now you don't seem connected.
I believed in your vision,
It was feeling so real.
I must have dreamt to hard,
Because it was a half-hearted deal.

Just Keeps Breaking

I feel the wind
I see the sun
I walk around dazed
And in circles
In this race that I run.
This life is so predicting,
No excitement at all
I'm unconscious and careless
But inside I am screaming.
What's tattered and torn
Is also shattered and broken
No love
No peace
And there's so much commotion.
I'm fighting but losing
I'm trying but failing
God help me,
I'm hopeless and crying.
I feel like I'm dying
Yet I'm doing just fine
You'd never know I was hurting
Unless you saw through my eyes.

Just Let Me Love You

Verse 1:

Baby you know my hearts been broken and beaten
You know I've had my tears
You know I've had my heartache
In the past few years

I've lived and loved
And I know how you feel
I don't to mean to look back
But these feelings are real

The past has been haunting me
But it won't anymore
I'm lost with you here
It's what I've waited for

Chorus:

Just let me love you baby
The way that I can
I wanna start over
For you to be my man

I know I've had rough times
But you're bringing me down
Down to your heart
Baby just let me drown

I've been tryin' so hard
I wanna to hold on
If love comes so easy
Why's it hard to stay strong?

So just let me love you
The way that I can
I wanna start over
For you to be my man
Just let me love you

Verse 2:

You're unsure about my feelings
But I assure you their true
My love's so much deeper
Now that I've found you

I know you think I'm joking
But just hear me out
My hurt can me mended
There's no need to doubt

I'm over the past
Show me the way
Give me your love
That's all I can say

Chorus:

Just let me love you baby
The way that I can
I wanna start over
For you to be my man

I know I've had rough times
But you're bringing me down
Down to your heart
Baby just let me drown

I've been tryin' so hard
I wanna to hold on
If love comes so easy
Why's it hard to stay strong?

So just let me love you
The way that I can
For you to be my man
Just let me love you

GIRLS

Little girls are full of laughter, hopes and wishes,
And even though they're young, dream of true love, hugs, and kisses.
Fairytales are acted daily, playing house, and defeating fiend,
Getting the prince, and becoming queen
They want to fit Cinderella's slipper, and have sleeping beauty's looks,
Kiss snow white's lover, and be every princess in the book.
They love to giggle and gossip; there open minded and willing to learn,
They give their love freely, and ask only to be loved in return,
Even when they're grown, they still have the same girly hopes they had,
They want true love, and never expect their story to end sad.
Their eyes still sparkle with fairytale dreams,
And deep down inside, they still believe,
They'll be loved by a prince, and live happily ever after,
Then they end up with the opposite, to have their hearts beat and shattered.
They did nothing wrong, just gave him their very soul,
They wished too hard, and his heart was cold.
Girls are always told to dream with all they have,
To have high expectations, and never settle for less.
Then we hope to high, and get our hearts broken by the best.

Let Me Go
(For him)

Verse 1:

I know it happened fast
I didn't mean for you to bleed so badly
And your still dwelling on the past

Did you think it was all just an act
When you saw me cry
And my heart ripped in two
When you told me goodbye

It's been long enough
Time to get off your knees
Save yourself now
I'm begging you please

Chorus:

Well I just wanted to tell you
It's ok to move on
And it's ok to let go
Cause I'm already gone

I just want you to be happy
Even though you're hurting
You can't keep on this way
It's your heart you're avoiding

You know I still cared for you
That's what pains you most
You put your pride above love
Now you can't hold me close

It hurts for me to see you this way
And it's very hard I know
But do me a favor
And let me go

Verse 2:

You can't keep hanging on like this
You have to dry your eyes
Pick up your broken pieces
And put away your disguise

I won't be responsible for the loss in your heart
You did that yourself
That's why we're apart

Let your wounds heal
Start smiling again
Let out your pain
And let forgiveness in

Chorus:

Well I just wanted to tell you
It's ok to move on
And it's ok to let go
Cause I'm already gone

I just want you to be happy
Even though you're hurting
You can't keep on this way
It's your heart you're avoiding

You know I still cared for you
That's what pains you most
You put your pride above love
Now you can't hold me close

It hurts for me to see you this way
And it's very hard I know
But do me a favor
And let me go

Let the Rain Just Fall

Verse 1:

I never used to drink,
I never tried to smoke,
But now that you walked away,
My heart has somehow broke.

When I finally realized I needed you
It was already to late
I tried to reach you again
But you just pulled away.

Chorus:

So let the rain just fall,
I've tried everything to get you back
And you still shut me out.

I'm givin' up,
I'm givin' in
To all the pain my heart is in.

Let if all as I cry
Against the windshield of my life,
Let it show all my sorrows
And all of my strife.

I'm not using any wipers
To stop this painful mood
This guilty attitude.

Verse 2:

I know you still love me,
So why do you stay away?
Ignore me like I'm just a friend,
Come on baby, we're more than that.

You stay busy
To keep from missin' me
But I know it ain't workin'
Cause the pain's in your eyes, can't you see?

But you won't come back
And that's what's killin' me,
Baby, I am what I am
That's all I can be.

Chorus:

So let the rain just fall,
I've tried everything to get you back
And you still shut me out.

I'm givin' up,
I'm givin' in
To all the pain my heart is in.

Let if all as I cry
Against the windshield of my life,
Let it show all my sorrows
And all of my strife.

I'm not using any wipers
To stop this painful mood
This guilty attitude.

Life

What is life but a moment?
That with one wrong touch,
Can slowly crumble in the palms of your hands.
What is life but a second?
It's here and then fades before your very eyes.
There is no time for grudges,
So let go and show forgiveness.
Love while you still live,
Before your time runs out;
For we are never promised tomorrow.

Life's Simple Pleasures

Sit on the front porch and let the bright sun surround you, wrapping you up in a warm embrace, like a grandmother who hugs her granddaughter. Lie on a blanket in the grass and stare at the stars as they twinkle like little fireflies in the darkness. Stand in the rain and let it trickle down your face and fingers, as it falls to the earths' soil. Play in the snow until your toes get cold, and then go inside for hot chocolate. Share your memories with your friends and family before they are forgotten. Life is short, so live it while you can.

Lizard Stew

(Ashleigh's first poem, written at 10 years of age)

I like lizard stew,
When it sits inside my shoe;
It has a sorta funny taste,
Kinda like paste.

I like lizard stew,
When it smells like the zoo;
It has a sorta funny smell,
Kinda like a fish's tail.

I like lizard stew,
Because it is the best;
Maybe if you're nice,
I'll give you all the rest.

But don't be afraid
Of what your most likely to find;
It's just little pieces of lizard,
Very well grind.

Look At Me Now

Verse 1:

You never look at me anymore,
Not even a glance as you walk on by,
It bothers you to,
And I think I know why.

You don't want me to see
All the sadness you let in,
You're afraid to break down,
You don't want to give in.

Chorus:

There's a gleam in your eyes
When you see me,
And a feeling that you need to be near me;
To look means to remember,
And to you, that would be to surrender;
To your broken heart,
Your hidden pain
And having only me to blame.
But look at me now
And let me see how much hurt you'll allow;
Look at me now.

Verse 2:

Well I'm hurting to,
As we fight our way through,
And it might let up some
If I got a glance from you.
But you're afraid to let me see your heart,
Even if I've seen it before;
Cause now that we're over,
You're afraid to want more.

Chorus:

Because there's a gleam in your eyes
When you see me,
And a feeling that you need to be near me;
To look means to remember,
And to you, that would be to surrender;
To your broken heart,
Your hidden pain
And having only me to blame.
But look at me now
And let me see how much hurt you'll allow;
Look at me now.

Love Changed My Heart

Love hath reached me from my darkest hour;
It brought me up
And gave me power.
My heart has changed,
And let me see;
Just how precious love can be.
That now I love,
And am loved in return,
A flame has risen,
And my soul now burns.

Love Found Me

I don't recognize this feeling,
What could it be?
If love feels like this
Has love really found me?

My heart feels like it's flying
And my soul is so content
He fills my life with joy
He must be heaven sent!

I think I've found my soul mate
Now I finally see
He's my one and only
Love has really found me!

Love is...

Love is a gift
To cherish and hold
Keep close to your heart
And more precious than gold.
Love is a treasure
We give to mankind
We give and receive it
In our hearts and our minds.
Love speaks so boldly
Yet says no words at all,
It helps us when hurt
And can help us when we fall.
Love is so sacred
And treated with care,
It's undying devotion
Is also so rare.
Yes, God gave us many gifts,
Many to recall,
But love is his greatest
The greatest of all.

Love is a Rose

The wilted rose that he holds in his hand is a memory of the lost love that had once devoured his heart, and left him breathless every time he thought about her. The memory had quietly slipped away from him in the darkness of one November night that would never leave his mind. The rose was a key to his future. Their future. But now that dream has died, along with the blood red rose that lay silently now on his lap.

I'm Back Where I've Never Been

Verse 1:

I've been living like love will never find me
Settling for just anyone so blindly
And I'd always act surprised when it didn't go right
Then you came along and shed some light
On my wondering mind

I've been living like soul mates don't exist
Always searching but somehow always miss
How did you find me when I'm so far away
How did you help me find all the words I needed to say

Chorus:

I'm right back where I've never been
But where I was always supposed to be
I'm right here in your loving arms
You've opened my eyes, let me see

I am someone who's never known that feeling
But I recognized it the moment it came so willingly
Like I was looking all along
And you knew right where I belonged

Verse 2:

Now I'm living because love has finally found me
And you've crept into my heart so soundly
Like you never were away
And it's just another day

Now I'm sure that soul mates do exist
I can feel it every time we kiss
Your love, it completes me
Because we were always meant to be

Chorus:

I'm right back where I've never been
But where I was always supposed to be
I'm right here in your loving arms
You've opened my eyes, let me see

I am someone who's never known that feeling
But I recognized it the moment it came so willingly
Like I was looking all along
And you knew right where I belonged

Moving On
(For Molly)

Verse I:

She lies awake again tonight
Her thoughts are so heavy
But she swears she's all right

She fights back the tears
Pours another glass of wine
Whispers to herself
"Just give it some time"

Chorus:
His bittersweet memories
Trip all over her heart
They're crooked and unforgiving
They are few and far apart

She's been on the hell side of love
And she's made it out alive
Faced heartache with a smile
And her spirit still survives

Verse II:

She turned her back on love
All it's done is leave her broken
There's a fence around her heart
And all these words she's left unspoken

Chorus:
And his bittersweet memories
Trip all over her heart
They're crooked and unforgiving
They are few and far apart

She's been on the hell side of love
And she's made it out alive
Faced heartache with a smile
And her spirit still survives

My Mood is Blue

Verse 1:

Oh, I'm tired from runnin'
Runnin' from somethin'
This thing called pain
That I'm feeling again.
I just want you to know,
That I miss you so bad,
I miss you to bad.

Chorus:

My mood is blue
My heart is gray;
I've done all I can do,
Since we've gone separate ways.

My life is dull,
My love is broken,
With all the hurtful words we've spoken.
And I wish you could see,
Oh I wish you knew;
That my mood is blue,
It's blue for you.

Verse 2:

I know I've done you wrong
But together is where you and I belong.
I know I hurt your pride,
But can't you see how I feel inside?
Cause I blame myself
For your departure
And I realize now,
I need you for sure.

Chorus:

My mood is blue
My heart is gray;
I've done all I can do,
Since we've gone separate ways.

My life is dull,
My love is broken,
With all the hurtful words we've spoken.
And I wish you could see,
Oh I wish you knew;
That my mood is blue,
It's blue for you.

My Only Plea
(For Molly)

Verse 1:

Here I am yet again lying wide-awake
Just for once, give me some peace for my souls sake

My tears go unheard, as they flee to the floor
I've cried so many, yet there always seems to be more

I feel like I'm broken and I'm falling so fast
Cause I'm stuck in the midst of our beautiful past

Chorus:

I'm drowning in a sea of your bittersweet memories
And I'm lost in a world that's full of my misery
You left me so cold, and now I'm just barely breathing
And I still feel my heart break, everyday that it's beating
But everything treasured is eventually lost
Just how much does your love really cost?
I can't close my eyes without your face there before me
Give back my happiness; it's my one and only plea

Verse 2

I'm walking in the circles that you left me behind
You tore me in pieces, and they're so hard to find

I would've tried not to love you, if I would have known
That I'd die every day, painfully alone

I believed in your lies, that you swore were the truth
I am the victim of your immature youth

Chorus:

I'm drowning in a sea of your bittersweet memories
And I'm lost in a world that's full of my misery
You left me so cold, and now I'm just barely breathing
And I still feel my heart break, everyday that it's beating
Everything treasured is eventually lost
Just how much does your love really cost?
I can't close my eyes without your face there before me
Give back my happiness; it's my one and only plea

My Summer Rose

When I was young and full of dreams
I met a boy, so perfect he seemed.
Beautiful and innocent was the love that we showed,
Held by the young
And envied by the old.
We were carefree and fearless
As the wild flower grows,
And I thought about you, my summer rose.

As we got older,
Our youth grew more wise,
The childhood love,
Turned into heartache and lies.
Parting was painful
And growing up hurt even worse
It seemed like love was nothing but a curse.
But it was the path that we chose,
And in time, I forgot you, my summer rose.

Years have passed by,
And I'm going through old things,
A poem was found, and what memories it brings.
Sitting by the stream, on a bed of smoothed stones,
How long we were there, only heaven knows,
And I remembered you, my summer rose.

My Tears Can't Always Run

Verse 1:

Yeah I bet you thought I'd hurt for months
After you said goodbye
That I'd bend so much I'd finally break,
And do nothing else but cry.

Well I'll have you know,
This heart can take
Much more than you cared to see;
Cause I haven't let go of a single tear
In the last few weeks.

Chorus:

Cause my tears can't always run,
Gotta save some to keep my sanity;
And the only thing I'm wonderin' now
Is what could've been with you and me.

And I'm just now movin' on
And my life have just begun,
I think of you from time to time,
But my tears can't always run.

Verse 2:

You probably thought I'd run and hide
And let my heart just suffer;
But I bet you didn't realize
I could ever love another.

Yeah it'll take awhile for love
To find it's way back here,
But in time I'll find
That I'm long gone
And your nothing left to fear.

Chorus:

Cause my tears can't always run,
Gotta save some to keep my sanity;
And the only thing I'm wonderin' now
Is what could've been with you and me.

And I'm just now movin' on
And my life have just begun,
I think of you from time to time,
But my tears can't always run.

Now I Miss You

I miss you already
And I don't know why,
But every time I try to start again,
Your face is all I see.
Your independence was so attracting,
And I longed so much to have it,
Your confidence was so great,
That I yearned to bask in it all.
I leaned on your shoulder,
And believed every word you ever spoke.
I know I was naïve,
But you seemed so perfect.
Now I sit alone,
With no one to run to,
And struggle to keep my own confidence alive.

One March Day
(For one of my best friends)

The sun's warm rays
beat down on my skin,
it's been six long months
and we're back there again.

A temporary seclusion
I'm nowhere but here;
I'm caught in this moment
and he still draws near.

There's so much emotion
we're alone in this world;
nothing but the sky,
this boy and this girl.

Love's to be feared
by first time believers,
his heart beats so fast;
he just wants to be with her.

But fear is a feeling
he pushed it away,
I'm lost in his arms
I'm lost in this day.

The warmth in his touch
the linger in his gaze,
his skin against mine
oh how I wanted to stay.

I run my fingers through his hair
and kiss him again,
we better get going
the day's gonna end.

Pillow of Tears

The tears are ever flowing
The sorrow is unknowing
Hold it in
Then let it out
The cloud will soak it up.
They run down the faces
In so many places
Streams and trickles
Drops in some cases.
Lay down for comfort
And let out your troubles
The pillow of tears
Will catch all your puddles.

Power of Love

Had love no power,
Life would cease;
What is living,
Without love's ease?

Life which has a caring soul,
Heeds love's calling,
Accepting as whole.

The hope of the world
Depends on its mercy;
Man's strong heart
Begs for its grace
So dear is life,
It longs for love's face.

Reach Those Days Again

Verse 1:

I was going through an old box of things
I found a yearbook and my senior ring
I held it up and smiled
And it took me back
To when I was half woman half child
It's amazing how something so small
Can bring me back to an entire lifetime
Where I held the world, I had it all

Chorus:

I had my first drink at seventeen
Fell in love somewhere in between
He broke my heart and left me there to cry
Didn't think I would ever pull through but I tried

I had good friends,
We have so many memories
Partied hard
Yeah I remember when that was me

When guy friends wanted to be more
And high school was a war
You tried to find out who you were
And love was never sure

Oh to reach those days again
When all you needed
Were a few good friends
Good wine,
And good men.

Verse 2:

The past is full of life
Laughter hopes and dreams
It's good to look back
No matter how far it seems
I'll lay the ring on my dresser for now
I wanna remember how....

Chorus:

I had my first drink at seventeen
Fell in love somewhere in between
He broke my heart and left me there to cry
Didn't think I would ever pull through but I tried

I had good friends,
We have so many memories
Partied hard
Yeah I remember when that was me

When you loved and you hated
Popularity was over rated
You tried to find your place in the world
Had to be like all the pretty girls

Oh to reach those days again
When all you needed
Were a few good friends
Good wine,
And good men.

Rejected Love

The love is true,
And destiny's found,
When broken hearts begin anew.
Trust is respected and honor is a must,
The two are one,
But some rejected.
As in a tale once told,
Their feelings held a key,
But the one's with power were withheld
It's love, but can't they see?
The past is done, the present's now,
Mistakes were made,
Don't make them run.

Rhythm of Life

Life has a rhythm. In every rhythm there's a beat. The beat of a heart, and the sound of children's feet. There's rhythm. In the laughter of a child, and in the cries of a suffering soul. There's rhythm. In a dance, in a song, in right or in wrong. There's rhythm. When the sun arises and when it falls, and in the brightest flower I ever saw. There's rhythm.

Season of Love
(for her)

Verse 1:

I've seen the wildflowers growing
And I've seen the fall leaves blowing
It changes every season
Without them ever knowing

Something was bloomin'
Beneath that old country sky
The small stream ripplin'
As the hours passed by.

Yeah a new season started
As they held each other close
To them there was no consequence
In the choice that they chose.

Chorus:

When a young girl gives her heart away
For the very first time,
Nothing can separate them
Their lost in each other's minds.
It was a season of love
And a season of change
When a girl becomes a woman
And can't get back what she gave away.
Oh to feel that way again,
A young heart's innocence, impatience and desire
Oh how it feels to feed love's first fire.

Verse2:

I remember my first time
Memories like just yesterday;
I come back here sometimes just to get away.
The sound of his voice
Is still in my head
Along with all the things he said.

Oh the way you feel
When your first in love,
Not knowin' it won't last,
It never does.

Chorus:

When a young girl gives her heart away
For the very first time,
Nothing can separate them
Their lost in each other's minds.
It was a season of love
And a season of change
When a girl becomes a woman
And can't get back what she gave away.
Oh to feel that way again,
A young heart's innocence, impatience and desire
Oh how it feels to feed love's first fire.

Set Our Love Free

I've loved so long
And now it falters
The pain is great,
But that soon will alter.
You set me free,
To love no more;
My heart has wings
And is ready to soar.
Still "I for you"
Will you desire,
But our love was fading,
And I grew tired.
If you're the one,
I'll never know
But if you love me,
Let me go.

Silent

I lay in the dark
The silence surrounds me
Alone and afraid
Is this how it has to be?

I can hear the rain pounding
And my heart beating loudly
I hate it so quiet
And there's no one to hold me

This feeling to empty
It hurts to be cold
So still in the darkness
I'll have to be bold

Not even a whisper
To calm my fears
The thoughts in my head
Are all that are here

Won't someone save me
Take me out of this hell
Hold my hand
Wake me out of this spell

Silent Security

Sitting here as the treetops sway,
Alone and secluded,
Inspiration for the day.
There are clouds in the sky,
It looks like rain;
Who knows where they're headed,
But Rita's to blame.
A gentle breeze flows through my hair,
The day is not promising,
It's not even fair.
It's gloomy,
Not sunny,
There's a chill in the air;
Every hour is forever,
But the day doesn't care.
It's quiet and lonely,
As a leaf flutters by;
The day has depressed me,
So I leave with a sigh.

She Touched Our Hearts

A little life born,
Yet the life not lived,
Conceived in sin,
But brought joy from within.
The time she had touched our lives,
Even from afar;
And though now gone from this world
Is always in our hearts.
So God we thank you for this tiny blessing,
Now and forever more,
For even in her death
Were you glorified,
For she was always yours.

We love you Alexis Jade MacIntire!!!!

Short poems for thought

1.) Your eyes are like two stars, twinkling in the moonlight. Your smile is like a rose, so sweet and gentle. You have the heart of a lion, and the voice a robin. Daring and courageous yet gentle with love and kindness.

2.) The clock ticks with every beat of his broken heart. The pain once felt so deep is now only a tingling numb. The bruise is still there; the reminder of his shattered dream is still vivid and alive. But hope is rekindling, as little as it may be, welling up in a pool of sorrow.

3.) The crisp morning air chills my skin as the first rays of light permeate me. My eyes adjust to the sudden change as I lean back and take it all in. The tall pines sway back and forth as they bend to the wind and their leaves rustle loudly in protest.

4.) What beauty embraces me as I stand and whirl in the bright light of day! The wind rushes through my veins like the very blood inside of me. The sun enflames me as a love for the soul.

Something to Live For

The stars are looking down,
And the moon has turned it's back;
This quaint uneasy feeling
And I'm falling to the ground.
The sky is black,
The clouds are gray,
I can't get back up
At the end of the day.
As deeper and deeper I fall,
There's no one here to stop me
And who knows what I saw.
I'm taken away in this dark misty place,
I'll keep on going, because my life is my race.

Southern Comfort

Sitting on the fencepost, I look out over the fields. The grass is swaying in the breeze, as the sun glistened like a million daytime stars on top of the lake. The stallion's mares graze about at various places in the lush greenery that surrounded them. Their own heaven. Leaves fluttered and rustled through the trees with the familiar sounds that rang often in my ears. All my life I have lived in these beautiful hills of grace and quietness of the country. Bees hovered over the many colorful flowers that clustered together, making the perfect pictures that you could only find here. This is the south. Yes, sitting here in the quietude of these peaceful hills calms and claims my soul.

Southern Solitude

Great towers overshadow me,
As I lay in a bed of colored leaves.
Here of my own will and not compelled at all.
Deeply hidden away,
And showered by a burst of warm sunshine.
An innocent breeze flows throughout the trees,
So I close my eyes as nature surrounds me.
The touch is so comforting,
My soul, fervently begs for more.
Slowly sitting up, I brush off the leaves from my shirt and smile.
I could be here forever,
But provoked by time,
I reluctantly rise and say my goodbyes.
He stomps his hooves loudly,
Telling me it's time to go,
So I hoist myself upwards
And peacefully ride into the fading sun.

Still Holding On

I thought that I'd be fine,
I thought I could let go
But week after week,
I've still no smile to show.

At your very last goodbye
I held my head up high
But here all alone,
I sit and I cry.

Every other moment,
I'm longing for your kiss
And all throughout the day
You're the only one I miss.
Now I'm all alone
And I hate to be alone,
And I never would have said those things
If I had ever known.

So hold me in your dreams
For that's where I now belong
I'll be there to touch your cheek,
And I'll whisper when I speak.
Now miss me more than ever,
Like you never have before
Miss me like I know you will
And I will too, for I love you still.

Support Our Troops

They threatened our country. They destroyed our families, so we fought back. We went to them to set them free from their persecutor; they didn't thank us. We caught their killer; they still hate us. We send our family and friends over to them. We fight for them everyday, and they still destroy us. They don't care. They think we are doing them wrong, when we only try to help. Now our own people hate it. They think we don't need to be there. They lose their hearts and lose sight of the importance in what we do. Our own families voice their disapproval. They are being selfish. They are disrespectful to those who fight for us. Our men lose their lives, while they sit and shake their head in foolish pride. God bless our troops.

Tell Me Love

Tell me love,
What do you see?
When your beautiful brown eyes
Look down upon me?

Do you see my love for you
Etched upon my face?
Or youthful lust
Full of tempting disgrace

Is there wrong
In this steamy bliss?
The surging heat
In a virgin's kiss?

Tell me love
Is this romance vain?
The passion I feel
Still left it's stain.

I tell you love,
I can't deny
Your body's plead
And the flame in your eye.

Tell me love,
Oh I wish you'd say
That you can't resist
You wish I'd stay

I tell you love,
I believe in this desire
This thirst for your heart
That sets my soul on fire.

The Lonely Loveless Road

What did I ever do to make you leave me
What did I ever say to make you go
The love was growing stronger every hour
But I guess you didn't feel the way I do

A single little rose
Broken by a storm filled word
A heart suddenly shattered
By a simple little phrase
And the tears began to flow
Down the lonely loveless road

I took the news fairly well
Cause I didn't want to cry in front of you
But when I was alone the hurt just hit me
Our memories flooded back into my soul

A single little rose
Broken by a storm filled word
A heart suddenly shattered
By a simple little phrase
And the tears began to flow
Down the lonely loveless road

You said that you still loved me
But I'm not sure that's true
Because the way I see it
I'd still be with you…

A single little rose
Broken by a storm filled word
A heart suddenly shattered
By a simple little phrase
And the tears began to flow
Down the lonely loveless road

The Man That Holds My Love

Verse 1:

It's finally five,
I'm gettin off work
Traffic's a mess
And I'm at my worst
I pull up the driveway
Throw my keys on the counter
The telephone rings
He asks if he can come over
He brings a smile to my face
On my longest days
His voice is like heaven
With his smooth talkin' ways

Chorus:

He's my knight in shining armor
When I feel trapped in a tower;
He's the hero of my heart
With no super natural powers

He's my shoulder to lean on
When I need a friend
My good dreams at night
That know no end

He's the fire in my soul
That can't be put out
The hug that surrounds me
That subsides all my doubt
Yeah he's the man I can't let go of
Cause he's the man that holds my love.

Verse II:

Another tear rolls down my face
A dead end road for the dream I chased
An empty feeling mocks me again
A hopeful prayer with no amen
But then he's there
Comes without a word
To wipe my red eyes
Where the teardrops blurred.

Chorus:

He's my knight in shining armor
When I feel trapped in a tower;
He's the hero of my heart
With no super natural powers

He's my shoulder to lean on
When I need a friend
My good dreams at night
That know no end

He's the fire in my soul
That can't be put out
The hug that surrounds me
That subsides all my doubt
Yeah he's the man I can't let go of
Cause he's the man that holds my love.

The Passion of Love

The sparkle of desire
Lingers in his eyes
While passion and love are compromised.

The warmth of his gaze
Lingers in his fingertips
While grace and beauty
Glaze his lips.

The softness of his words
Whisper in my ear
While promises are made
And he draws near.

The Truth That I Owe

Verse 1:

I woke up this morning
Having dreamt of you,
It opened my eyes,
And then I knew;
That I've lied to myself,
And I've cheated my heart.
I should've known we weren't meant to be apart.

Chorus:

Cause I'm stuck in our memories
And I can't set you free,
Your trapped in my heart,
And I can't find the key.

I've tried to find love
But I just can't let go
Of the promise you gave me
And the truth that I owe.

Verse 2:

Well it's all my fault,
Cause I made myself believe
That I needed something more,
But now I see…

Chorus:

That I'm stuck in our memories
And I can't set you free,
Your trapped in my heart,
And I can't find the key.

I've tried to find love
But I just can't let go
Of the promise you gave me
And the truth that I owe.

Together Alone

It's ten after two,
I'm looking at you
You stroke my hair
And lift my chin
I tell you
I know just where to begin

Suddenly we find ourselves
Torso to torso
Skin to skin
I held him tight
And I saw him grin

His lips brushed mine
I accept and go on
Ever the deeper
All hesitance gone

His fingers tickle my side
I close my eyes
He tilts my head back
And I'm facing' the sky

A kiss on the neck
And I'm lost in this bliss
A contented sigh
Man, I love this…

Trail of Tears

Along this path my life now leads,
We are bound in our bodies
In our hearts we are free.
Taken are our hands
My feet are forced to move
Depression overwhelms us
Yet my spirit still withstands
A part of life they say it is
A different road we follow
But this can't be right
I wonder if they know.
Gone are many along this path
A fault that's not our own
Taken and broken
With no love to be shown

Tragedy of the Soul

What is this tension
That's making me bleed
These hardcore emotions
And the relief that I need

My life's so uncertain
I'm about to give in
I'm going to break,
Lord, I'm back here again

I'm falling so hard
Someone give me your hand
Help me get off my knees
And help me to stand

Will this ever feel right?
Or am I hoping to high
To have someone here hold me
That won't just feed me lies

I feel so much
And still nothing at all
No one here cares
And yet they all saw

The numbness will calm me
I'm all right for now
God this has to get better
But I just can't see how

Troubled Life

She walks into the room and I stare at her, trying to figure her out. What secrets does her heart hold deep inside. The story of her life. Not yet sixteen and she pretends she's under control. That nothings wrong. She hides herself behind black, like she's wrapped up in sin and no one knows her pain. She goes to her friends, but she is nothing by herself. She's reclusive as she seeks truth and understanding. Trying to search within herself, she looks so deep but misses the entire point. Or does she want to see it?

True Love

These that love
And shalt remain;
With hearts entwined,
And a lover strain.
Neither life nor death
Shall come between,
A lover's heart
And the passion seen.
As life's light dwindles
And desire's their aim,
These loves never falter,
They're always the same.

Unsaved Death

I could feel it. It surrounded me like a blanket that was wrapped around me too tightly. The eerie sense of death crawled across the room, coming and waiting to claim it's next victim, and carry them to the immortal world. It's something that you can't stop, and it won't stop once it begins. When your time comes, you will experience the awful cries that you hear when you're at the end of your last thread that keeps you connected to this world. I can feel it coming. It's cold and I can't stop shivering. It haunts you like it's laughing at you because you have no control over it. It wants you. I lay there with sweat drops of pain trickling down my forehead as it rests heavily on my chest. Now I know that God is real. But now it's too late.

Unspoken

A life had once been lived
With secrets of shame,
And the hidden past had nothing to give.
Long ago,
The lies are unknown,
But thoughts are still remembered;
Why did this happen?
She must have been shown.
Lost memories occur,
They're haunting each breath;
Nobody can know,
Not even in death.
What's happened back then,
She still isn't told,
But there's pain and lost feelings
She's hidden like gold.

Untitled

Look at that young woman,
Walking through those church doors,
She's got a smile on her face
To hide all her disgrace.
Another given Sunday,
She's fooled them again;
A born again Christian,
Hiding all her new sin.

She left the only man she really loved
And cheatin' on the one she's with now,
She's trying to stop,
But she doesn't know how.
Her mind is a cloud,
And she can't see clearly;
She's trying to walk straight,
But her heart is so dreary.

We Got Wheels

Verse I

I'm a blonde headed girl
I got blue eyes,
and southern pride
pretty simple minded,
Take it easy, most of the time.

She was a prom queen nominee,
Pretty as she can be,
Most call her molly,
But it's cousin to me

We can be shy
In our everyday lives
Try to go unnoticed
Until we get to drive.

Chorus:

 But put us together,
And it's good girls gone wild
Give us something to steer
And it's trouble with a smile
If it's just cruisin' down the interstate
Windows down and music loud,

Shades, and Taylor Swift is all we need
Talkin' bout heartaches,
and laughin' bout that "perfect man" breed;
hangin' out the window
and waving at the guys
givin' it some gas
with mischief in our eyes;
yeah it's surprising we ain't got the cops on our heels
when we got wheels!

Verse II

I'm pretty much an introvert
Keep to myself, so I don't get hurt
Watch what I say, and watch what I do
I procrastinate a lot before I see things through

She's had her share of heartbreaks
She's got a fence around her heart
She thinks things out before she ever starts
Got a good head on her shoulders
And won't let just anyone hold her

We're a few good women
Until we get behind that steering wheel
Then we're carefree and fearless
We'd strike em' dead
If good looks could kill

Chorus:

But put us together,
And it's good girls gone wild
Give us something to steer
And it's trouble with a smile

When it's four wheelers
And dirt piles,
Ball caps and muddy niles
Makin fun of "ex's"
And trashin' their name for awhile

We're crazy out loud
when we wanna be seen
beautiful rednecks,
countrified teens;
yeah the boys are always on our heels
when we got wheels!

What Did You Gain

Verse 1:

You're falling harder every time
You finally see your wrong
You let me go so easy
When you really wanted to hold on

It seemed like you weren't bothered
You slept fairly well at night
Your pride was held in tact
But your heart was in a fight

You tried to stay away
But you were always around
You had to see for yourself
Watch me get off the ground

But what you saw
You didn't like
It broke your heart
A hidden strike

Chorus:

You watched me fall to pieces
Day by day
You were terribly close
And so far away

You listened to my silent weeping
And still you didn't show
Close enough to hear me cry
But at a distance so no one would know

Did you enjoy to see me suffer?
All those months of pain
You act like nothing happened
Tell me, what did you gain?

What did you gain?

Verse 2:

Now you can't forget
All those painful memories
Now I've moved on
And you still can't see

Your haunted by your pride
You're angry with yourself
You didn't try to reach me
And I'm fine by myself

Couldn't you hear me screaming?
I wanted to feel you catch me
Waiting with open arms
For you to hear my plea

Chorus:

But you just:
Watched me fall to pieces
Day by day
You were terribly close
And so far away

You listened to my silent weeping
And still you didn't show
Close enough to hear me cry
But at a distance so no one would know

Did you enjoy to see me suffer?
All those months of pain
You act like nothing happened
Tell me, what did you gain?

What did you gain?

When You Think of Fayetteville

Verse 1:

You can't tell me your not hurting
Cause I can see it in your eyes;
Everywhere you've been is a memory
Full of my love,
And your lies.

Chorus:

So when you think of Fayetteville,
You'll think of me.
The razorback theatre,
And the movie we went to see.
You'll think of the love we found
In the country club pool,
And you'll hear that song by Buddy Jewel.
And you'll think of me.

Verse 2:

We've been together so long,
You're not over me yet,
So don't try to fool me,
I know your memories won't let you forget.

Chorus 2:

Cause when you think of Little Rock
You see our favorite spot
And your big ole truck
Parked in the Wal-Mart lot
And you think of our picnic,
And my favorite pair of jeans,
And you hear my favorite songs
By Pat Green and Billy Dean.
And you'll have no choice
But to think of me.

Verse 3:

You can run,
But you can't hide,
You still know you lied;
You let me go
So now I'm gone
You're out of my heart
But I'm still in your mind.

Chorus 3:

So when you think of Branson,
You'll think of me,
All out time spent together
And how we were meant to be.
You'll hear me laugh
And feel my lips,
But it will all be a dream,
And you'll think of me.

Who Are You

Who are you to say we're through?
And our love's no longer there?
I don't believe you know my heart,
Or know how much I care.

Who are you to say we're through?
And our love has died away?
I don't believe you know my soul,
So there's nothing you can say.

Only you can say YOU'RE through,
And that YOU'RE love has faded,
But as for me, my love is true
And that cannot be jaded.

So here we are, you say we're over,
But it's not you who gets to choose…
Cause only I can change my heart…
…Okay, I guess we're through.

Why?

Why is it so hard to stay true?
You know who love
And you know who you hate,
But why is it hard to stay true?

The flirting,
The playing
It's all a big lie;
To boost up your confidence
To keep your spirit alive.

Some call this a certain name,
I call it insecure;
Someone shows interest
And you'll play along for sure.

So why is it so hard to stay true?
A lack of self-assurance
And thinking everyone's better than you.

Wild Majesty

He walks like a prince
He prances like a prize,
He gallops with such strength
And runs with long majestic strides.
His nostrils are flared
His forelocks in his face,
His muscles work at a graceful pace.
He floats like an angel
As he runs o'er the plain
His head is held with pride
With his white wispy mane.
His long flowing tail
Sails ever so high
It's reaching up
To touch the sky.
His hooves beat like heartbeats
Fast with a fury
As they collide with the ground
Yet they're not in a hurry.
He's as graceful as a king
As he dances under the sun
And his name is called
The Wild One.

Wings

Verse 1:

Well I remember the summer of 2005
The love you helped me find,
We felt so alive.
We stood together like soul mates
We had stars in our eyes,
So when you said you had to go,
It took me by surprise.

I didn't know why,
And I didn't understand,
How something so perfect
Slipped right through my hands.

Chorus:

You gave me wings
When I wasn't ready to fly
And put my heart on a road
That left me all alone.
You left me hanging for one last kiss,
How could you just leave me like this?

Verse 2:

That one night in August,
In the woods by the creek;
The moon was so bright
As he started to speak.
I made a mistake
That only God saw
My innocence gone
As the leaves started to fall.

When daddy found out
And looked at the test,
His face looked so hard
As he made a fist.
I was forced to pack my bags
And get out on my own,
I wasn't ready for a child,
I should've known.

Chorus 2:

He gave me wings
When I wasn't ready to fly
And put my feet on a road
That left me all alone
He pushed me away
When I needed him most
Pregnant and guilty
As I headed for the coast.

Verse 3:

Well my baby's grown up now
And she's walkin down the isle;
She's glowing like an angel
As I see her start to smile.
That's boy's up there waiting
To take her by the hand
They've waited so long
For that wedding band.

I'm so happy for her
As I let go of a tear;
Her happiness means everything to me,
That's why we are here.

Chorus 3:

I gave her wings
When she was ready to fly
And put her heart on a road
That would always lead her home;
I'll be here to hold her
As the years go by
They walk back down the isle
And I started to cry.

Winnin' the Fight
(For Molly)

Verse 1:

Well he's done it again
He's let her go
And he won't forget it
Cause she'll let him know

She'll let him know
That he did her wrong
Shove it in his face
How she waited so long

And all he'll see
Is her movin' on
So when he starts to miss her
She'll already be gone

Yeah you better watch out:
Cause she's got you beat now boy,
And she might be cryin' tonight
But all you see is her movin on
And right now she's winnin' the fight

Chorus:

It's time to show that boy
What a woman will do
When he breaks her heart
And tears it in two

She'll call up all her girlfriends
And they'll head out to town
Dress up so sexy
And let her hair down

Yeah she'll drink it up
And party loud
Laugh till it hurts
And show off to the crowd

She'll be dancin' real hot
And smilin' real sly
She's havin' some fun

Since you told her goodbye
She's got you beat now boy
And she might be cryin' tonight
But all you see is her movin on
And right now she's winnin' the fight

Verse 2:

Yeah I bet you see now
That you're a quitter
What were you thinking'?
Heaven forbid
You fall in love with her

But she'll be all right
At least that's what you see
Man she's good at this game
There's a difference in
"Break up and defeat"

Chorus:

It's time to show that boy
What a woman will do
When he breaks her heart
And tears it in two

She'll call up all her girlfriends
And they'll head out to town
Dress up so sexy
And let her hair down

Yeah she'll drink it up
And party loud
Laugh till it hurts
And show off to the crowd

She'll be dancin' real hot
And smilin' real sly
She's havin' some fun
Since you told her goodbye

She's got you beat now boy
And she might be cryin' tonight
But all you see is her movin on
And right now she's winnin' the fight.

With You

Within myself
No soul can find
For in your heart
I now confide

My tears
Like rain
Make pools when pained
Which your love
Like grace
Keeps contained.

The comfort found
Not one can match
And your loving arms
Are meant to catch

The words not spoken
Yet speak so great
Yours and mine
It's not just fate

Your eyes like stars
Lead me away
To a place far better
Than mouths can say.

You Lied

You said I was yours,
You said that you were mine,
I gave you my heart,
And you lied.

I kissed you goodnight,
I hugged you tight,
I told you my past,
And you lied.

We were oh so in love,
And you made me cry,
You had hold of me,
And you lied.

You said that you loved me,
We were perfect, and right,
You let go of my hand,
Because you lied.

You Linger No More

You let me go,
And told me no,
And said that I'd be fine;
A temporary release,
To an impulsive decision;
You played with my heart,
And made a permanent incision.
We should give it a break,
And just see how it goes,
Well baby, I'm gone,
And that just goes to show,

You linger no more,
Your shadow is gone,
No more dark nights;
I stand in the dawn.
I let you go,
And pushed you aside,
Threw away your old memories;
And wiped away tears that I cried.

You Never Liked It

Verse 1:

You never liked my cowboy boots,
My cowgirl hat,
Or my rebel flag tattoo.
You never liked my horse,
Or the country side of me;
But something about it
Drew you closer to me.

You said you didn't like my wilder side,
But you could never stay away;
You'd always argue no,
Yet you'd kiss me just the same.

Chorus:

But you liked the way I walked
When I wore those cowboy boots,
And you liked the pride in my southern roots
When I showed you my tattoo.
You liked the way I tipped my hat,
And gave you that "come here baby" look.
One touch left you captivated
And then you were hooked.
You loved the way looked
When I'd fly across the field
And the way that I kissed you
Leaning up off my heels.

Verse 2:

You denied likin' it all
But you loved me anyway,
You held me the same
Despite all you'd say.

You'd tell me again
How you hated my southern side
And I'd remind you again
How often you tried to hide…

Chorus:

That you like the way I walk
When I wear these cowboy boots,
And you like the pride in my southern roots
When I show you my tattoo.
You like the way I tip my hat,
And give you that "come here baby" look.
One touch leaves you captivated
And then you're hooked.
You love the way look
When I fly across the field
And the way that I kiss you
And lean up off my heels.

Your Death Carries Me On

I'm losing my mind
I see you in the halls
I keep on looking
But never can find.
I can't believe your gone
But your death carries me on.

I cry every night
And fall asleep with your picture
The house is so lonely
My emotions are a mixture
I still can't believe your gone
But your death carries me on.

I got fired from work
And my heart cries out in pain
But my memories of you
Keep me from going insane.
The world is no more
No one stands beside me
I'm not doing well
As you can plainly see.
Your gone, but I'll be ok
Because you carry me on.

Your Love is Addicting

Verse 1:

What are these emotions baby
Running through my head,
It's been so long,
And I've moved on,
And I don't remember what I said.

But honey lately I can't sleep,
And my bed just feels so empty;
And I don't know why calling you now,
Is really very tempting.

Chorus:

Baby I can't help it,
But lately you've been on my mind
I don't know why
Your love is so easy to find.
But your memory won't leave me
No matter how hard I try,
I know my heart's someone else's
And that's what makes me cry.
I shouldn't miss you like this,
But you won't let me go
Your heart still holds me,
Trust me, I know.

Verse 2:

My hurt's been mended,
My love's been avenged,
But we had something going,
And I think of you every now and again.

Chorus:

Baby I can't help it,
But lately you've been on my mind
I don't know why
Your love is so easy to find.
But your memory won't leave me
No matter how hard I try,
I know my heart's someone else's
And that's what makes me cry.
I shouldn't miss you like this,
But you won't let me go
Your heart still holds me,
Trust me, I know.

www.ingramcontent.com/pod-product-compliance
Lightning Source LLC
Chambersburg PA
CBHW030520100426
42813CB00001B/95